Arthur
in Venice

For my mother, who helped me discover this magnificent city
For Dominique, Anouck, Tibaut
For Laura, Tibor, Antoine

*If you want to visit Venice and do Arthur's tour with a professional guide, we warmly recommend VENICE KIDS TOUR. Reserve your tour at **www.venicekidstours.com**. Your visit will take on quite another dimension.*
With special thanks to guide Rossana COLOMBO who has shared her knowledge and has revealed to us this fantastic city through interesting stories.

Titles of the same series
Arthur in Genève
Arthur in Londres
Find them at www.arthurvoyage.ch

Arthur in Venice
First published, 2019 by Grace Note Publications.
Grange of Locherlour, Ochtertyre,
Crieff, Scotland, PH7 4JS, UK

www.gracenotepublications.co.uk
books@gracenotereading.co.uk

ISBN 978-1-913162-09-2

Original version *Arthur à Venise*
Original text © Caroline Ferrero-Menut 2019
Illustrations © Nicole Devals 2019

Translator Susy Macaulay 2019

All reproduction prohibited without the author's permission.

A catalogue record for this book is available from the British Library

Arthur
in Venice

Caroline Ferrero Menut

Illustrator Nicole Devals

GNP

Travelling has always been my dream, so when I found out I had the amazing secret power of travelling in my dreams, I thought of only one thing: when would I set off? Where would I go? But everything turned out very differently from how I had imagined....

Chapter I
Elio

This journey has a special place in my heart because of my travel buddy, who helped me discover this city full of surprises.

I'm sure you also have a little teddy, a doll or something else you've been carrying around since you were small, and which means a lot to you.

For me, it was Elio. So who on earth is Elio? you're asking yourself.

Guess. He has a thick mane.

No, it's not a horse….

OK, here's a clue- he roars. Yes, you've got it this time- Elio is a lion.
A cute little lion with soft fur, and I sleep with him every night.

I love him so much because he's a bit mysterious: Elio has wings!
Have you ever seen a lion with wings?

Because I'm curious, I asked everyone round about for an explanation, my parents, friends, and even our teacher. They all laughed and made fun of me, but no one has ever been able to tell me why this lion has wings.

But I was convinced there was an explanation.

Chapter 2
My Punishment

One day I was in a very bad mood. The teacher had given me a punishment exercise because as she said, 'you don't know how to keep quiet!'

I was a bit scared of going home. My parents are nice, but when it comes to school, they don't mess around, I must always behave perfectly. I knew I was in for a bad time.

I wasn't wrong, children know these things….I had to do my punishment exercise, and once they had told me off, my mother gave me a bowl of soup and my father ordered me straight to bed, in front of my brothers and sisters who were falling about laughing.

I did what I was told without a word, but I was furious. A punishment at school, a punishment at home, this was too much for one day. I slipped under the covers and looked for Elio. I squeezed him tightly to my chest, crying quietly so that no one would hear me. Elio had been the recipient of plenty of tears over the years.

I shared all my troubles with him and he always managed to make me feel better. I snuggled up to him, my nose in his fur so I could smell him.

My eyes were drooping with tiredness and tears. I was on the point of falling asleep when I heard a voice calling out to me.

"Arthur, don't be so sad."

I was so surprised I leapt in the air.

"Who's that calling me, who are you?"

"Come on, don't you recognise me although I've been with you every single day for years?"

"If this is a joke, it's not very funny! I'm going to scream!"

"Oh Arthur, don't be afraid, it's me, Elio."

"Elio? My Elio?"

"Oh yes my friend, I've always been here for you and today I'm going to give you a surprise."

I looked at my lion, still squeezing him in my arms. He looked like he always looked, only – it was a bit strange, his mouth opened and shut and sounds came from it.

Wide awake and not upset anymore, I said:

"Elio, you can speak, that's amazing!"

"Yes, and I can do lots of other things, come on, follow me."

Chapter 3
The flight

I was asking myself where on earth could he go, that little lion with the furry paws, when something even more amazing happened. Elio was flying, he had opened his wings and was flying around me without the least difficulty.

I watched him open-mouthed.

"Shut your mouth or you'll swallow a fly, and follow me, you can fly too."

Sometimes, you have to know when not to ask questions and to make the most of the situation. I lifted the covers and immediately shot up into the air.

"Come on," Elio, who was already well away, shouted over to me. "I'll take you on a journey."

I flew out of the window with no fear of crashing into it, and followed him.

My body was light and did everything I wanted, a bit like when you're in water. I didn't even ask Elio where we were going, it didn't matter, I was flying, through clouds, alongside birds, I was flying!

There was a long quiet spell as the sun rose, turning the sky pink. Elio slowed down and said:

"We'll be there soon, shut your eyes and let yourself be carried along, it's important that you get the element of surprise."

I gave him my hand without hesitation, and sensed we were landing. Elio went on:

"Wait a bit, there you go, sit down and PAY ATTENTION, one, two three… open your eyes!"

Slowly, I opened my eyes and there in front of me was Elio's city.

Chapter 4
A little piece of paradise

We perched together on the roof of a big building, and what I saw was so strange, I just sat there without saying anything, taking in the spectacle.

The sun was nudging above the horizon, the sky was full of pale pink reflections, and the city was slowly beginning to wake up. But in this town, water had replaced streets, and boats had replaced cars. Yes, really!

There were already lots of people about and I watched what they were doing closely. Some of them looked like they were heading to work and they got into the motorboats like you would get on a bus at home. Fruit and vegetable sellers went around in boats. And then there were the men standing up on long black boats, pushing them along with a sort of oar.

I sat in silence for a long time, watching this unbelievable landscape, and I told myself how cool it must be to live here, on the water, even if it made grazing the cows and sheep more complicated!

I turned to Elio and asked him:

"Where are we? I've never heard of a city on water, it's so beautiful…"

Elio was quiet, motionless, also making the most of a scene which seemed to absorb him completely. He turned towards me.

"This is my town, Artie, this is VENICE."

"VENICE? That rings a bell, wait, oh yes, Venice Italy, I read it was the city of lovers!"

"True, they do say that, because of the magic of the water. Wait and see, I'm going to show you round, and there will be plenty more surprises. We're sitting on the roof of the station, and in front of you is the Grand Canal, the main 'street'" -he laughed- "in Venice. We could continue flying over the city, but that would be a shame. We're going to copy the tourists and take the boat, follow me!"

"But Elio, what will people say when they see a lion and a child flying about and travelling together alone on a boat?"

"No-one will see us Arthur, we're invisible. You can see me and I can see you, that's it. I told you you'd like the trip."

Chapter 5
We set sail…

I followed him and we landed on one of the banks of the Grand Canal, not far from the station. We climbed into a motorboat where lots of passengers were already aboard.

"This is a vaporetto boat, it serves the city a bit like a bus, making regular stops on one side or the other of the Grand Canal. It's still a bit chilly, do you want to go inside?"

"Oh no Elio, let's stay outside, I want to see absolutely everything, and breathe in the very air of your home town."

We sat down and sailed down the Grand Canal for more than half an hour. Elio told me that not only was Venice built on water, but what's more it's shaped like a fish, split down the middle by the Grand Canal, where we were. I found that funny.

We sailed gently along, looking at the scenery. There are lots of bridges, about 450 according to Elio, who grabbed me by the arm and shouted:

"St Mark's Square, everyone off!"

We had come to a huge square, already full of people and….pigeons. Dozens, hundreds, thousands of pigeons. I began running about behind them and Elio followed me. It was so funny, because we were invisible to the others, but the pigeons flew off when we ran behind them. We roared with laughter.

"Wait," said Elio. "Come on, let's have a bit of fun."

He picked some yellow grains up off the ground, spread my arms out and put some grain on each of my hands and my head. In a split second, I was covered… in pigeons: they sat on my hands, on my head to eat the grain while I laughed out loud and Elio ran round me.

Once the pigeons had flown off, Elio signaled to me to follow him.

"We're going to climb that big tower you see over there, called the Campanile. It's the first building to be built on the square, and it's 98 meters high. The Italians call it affectionately 'il padrone de casa'.

"What does that mean?"

"It means The Boss, because as you can see, it seems to be keeping watch over the whole square. But you know, a very long time ago, in 1902, the tower collapsed."

"Oh no, was anyone killed?"

"Only one death, and you'll never guess what…. a cat! Don't make that face, it hasn't fallen down since! Let's go up!"

Luckily, there was a lift. We reached the top in a few minutes. From up there, we could see all the roofs in Venice, and St Mark's Square from up in the sky was even more impressive.

"Elio, I was just thinking as we went up in the lift- how is it that you come from Venice, you don't look very Italian," I said mockingly.

"Clever clogs, you're making fun of me, so you'll just have to find out all by yourself why Venice is my town."

I had annoyed him. He went off to the lift, and we went down in silence.

"Look closely at the basilica of Saint Marc, clever clogs, and you will find a clue to answer your earlier, intelligent question."

"The basilica? What's that? I know 'basil' but not basilica!"

"Numbskull, don't they teach you anything in school? A basilica is a church."

Chapter 6
Elio's secret

I went inside the church. It was just so big. The cupolas on the ceiling were covered in gold, the floor beneath us was made of different sorts of coloured stones put together like a pretty puzzle. I thought to myself how amazing men are, to have made such huge churches with their own bare hands.

But I still couldn't see where Elio could have come from. Nothing in this church made me think of him. I would have thought Elio came from Africa, and here there were no gazelles or antelopes.

He was waiting for me out in the square when I came out.

"You're having me on, Elio, you know I didn't find anything. Give me a clue!"

"All right, let's go for a stroll on St Mark's Square, go round the church and you should find clues about me, Mr Clever Clogs."

Curious, I started walking and it wasn't long before I got what Elio meant. In front of the church there were two tall things like wooden masts stuck in the ground and on top of each one- a little lion. On the left of the basilica, a tower with a magnificent clock, and on the top a lion with one paw resting on an open book. Behind the church, we came to a square called 'Lion Square', which had two very beautiful stone lions. I asked Elio:

"Why does Venice have all these lions?"

"You haven't seen them all yet. There are tens of lions right in St Mark's Square. And look over there, the Venetian flag."

"Another lion, unbelievable! Would you please explain? And why do all these lions have wings, like you?"

"Ah, it's a long story. It's likely that the early Venetians, who travelled a lot by boat because the sea is very close, would have brought back the first statue from their travels in the Orient. "They say this statue had the body of a lion, a face more like a man than an animal, and wings. So the lion was chosen by the Venetians as a symbol of the courage and strength of their town. It's also the animal which represents St Mark, the saint who gave his name to the square. "And to this day, it's the lion which honours the best films from the Venice Film Festival, you know, the famous 'golden lion.'"

"How very strange. So you do actually come from Venice?"

"Yes, a lady bought me in a shop over there, and took me to your house. But that's enough wasting time with explanations, let's take a gondola tour of the canals, you'll see, it's magic. Come on, jump in, this one's free."

Chapter 7
The Gondola

We settled down in one of the superb black boats I'd seen when we arrived, and the gondolier, who couldn't see us of course, sang a song in Italian while he paddled along with his one oar.

Without a word we drifted along, and time seemed to stand still. The soft slap of the water lulled us as we took in our dream-like surroundings.

All of a sudden Elio made me jump, saying:

"Don't nod off, Arthur, I've got lots of things to show you. Look, we're going under the Bridge of Sighs."

"The Bridge of Sighs?"

"Yes, it's called that because in the olden days, this bridge linked the courts that you can see on the upper floors of the Doges Palace on your left, with the prison over there on your right. So crossing this bridge was the last moment of freedom for prisoners who had been imprisoned for life, or for many years."

"So, of course they sighed…"

"Yes. But nowadays, legend has it that if you kiss someone under the Bridge of Sighs, you'll be happy for ever."

"OK, let's go Elio, one, two, three, SMOOOOCH, with a kiss is big as this, we should be happy for the rest of our lives."

We both laughed, feeling so happy together, friends forever in this town so full of surprises.

Chapter 8
Through the streets of Venice

Reluctantly we disembarked from the gondola, and Elio led me up the steps of the Doge's Palace.

"Look, another lion."

A lion's head sculpted on a wall, mouth open, and inside its mouth a hole like the ones for posting letters in a post box.

"Strange, what's that for?"

"It was very useful back in the day. It's called a 'bocca di leone', lion's mouth."

"But what was it for? It looks like a post box.'

"Almost. In the past, people who collected taxes worked in this building, and 'the mouth' was there for people to tell on their neighbours for cheating and not paying their taxes."

"Oh, nice people around here! You know at school, if you tell on someone you're bound to get a doing."

Elio smiled and we left for a stroll down the little alleys towards St Mark's Place.

"I'm going to show you a little bookshop, and then let's go for a bite to eat. You can't leave here without having an ice cream and choosing a lovely cake."

"Now there I couldn't agree with you more."

We came to the bookshop. It was really amazing. I went in and couldn't stop smiling: there were books everywhere, but not like in a library or normal bookshop. Here, they were stacked in surprising places: a bath in the middle of the shop and also in a real gondola, it was like being in a cave full of books, with a few cats too, sleeping in the midst of all these piles.

"It's mind-blowing. I could spend the whole day here."

"Yes, me too," Elio replied. " Look, you come right into the shop by boat, and when the water level goes up in the rain, the bookshop gets full of water. That's why the books are in a gondola or a boat to protect them. Come and see the little courtyard inside, see, they've even made a staircase out of books so you can look down from up there."

I was truly amazed, and we left the bookshop grinning from ear to ear. I hadn't forgotten that we had decided to have a snack, and for me eating is always the most important thing.

First of all we went to a 'gelateria' where there were flavours of ice cream I'd never seen before. I found it very difficult to choose between all the beautiful, mouthwatering colours.

Then we went into a cake shop and Elio said:

"I'm going to be the one to choose here, because you should taste our specialities. We're going to have 'bussolai', those S-shaped biscuits, you see? They're in the shape of the Grand Canal."

We sat down at the water's edge and ate our ice creams and lemon flavor biscuits. Delicious, we felt so good.

I told Elio:

"I love your town, I could live here. You must be sad to have left it."

"No, I'm not sad, because that's how I found you. Now I have a friend, and that's so important. I'm not on my own anymore and I can always come back if I want, with you, my friend."

I squeezed him really hard. I was so happy to have him too, and proud that he thought it was more important to be with me than to live in Venice.

Chapter 9
Help, I'm lost!

We started strolling again in the streets of Venice. I was a bit tired, and stopped for a minute to look at some carnival masks.

One of them caught my eye- it was completely white, plain and had a long nose. It was on a mannequin dressed in a long white robe and white gloves. I wondered what on earth it could mean.

Just then, a little girl with freckles came in the shop, and started looking at the same mask as me. I followed her and heard her asking the assistant:

"That disguise, who is it?"

"Ah now that, my dear young lady, is a very famous disguise. The plague doctor.

"The plague doctor?"

"Oh yes. In Venice at that time there was lots of disease and serious epidemics. So to keep from catching the bugs, doctors put on this weird mask and thought they were safe. Some of them even filled the long nose with perfumes and medicinal herbs to protect themselves, and not smell the bad stink."

I turned to the girl and said:
"Super cool disguise. Those doctors were pretty smart!"

But of course, she didn't see or hear me. I left the shop and went in search of Elio.
I looked right, I looked left- no one. My heart began to pound.

I shouted at the top of my voice:

"Elio, Elio, I'm over here. Where are you?"

No answer, and I still couldn't see him. People passed by in the alley without reacting. I was frightened. Without Elio I was lost, I didn't know Venice and I was only a child. How would I get home? I didn't know the way, and I wasn't even sure I would know how to fly again. My throat tightened.

I carried on haphazardly down the alleyways, following tourists as they strolled about. I reached a little square, from which there was a beautiful bridge in white stone over the Grand Canal. I read what it said on the plaque I found next to me: 'Rialto Bridge'.

I thought if I climbed to the top of the bridge, I could get a better view of the town and perhaps have a better chance of finding Elio. I climbed the stairs four at a time, there were lots of shops on each side of the bridge, and the tourists formed one great mass, which made my search more difficult.

Once I got to the top, I looked down the Grand Canal, right, left, no one. From one side of the bridge to the other. No one.

My journey couldn't possibly end like this. Venice was far too magnificent a city for me to be lost, crying, abandoned amid hundreds of people who couldn't see me.

So I climbed onto the edge of the bridge and shouted with all my strength: "Elio,

Eliooooooooooooooo!"

Then I jumped when I heard a voice right by my ear:

"Stop shouting like that, I'm here, your very own Elio."

Chapter 10
Going home

I opened my eyes, not having a clue where I was. My mother was by the side of my bed holding Elio.

"Aren't you a bit too big to yell like that because you lost your cuddly toy? Elio's here, at the foot of your bed. You could have kept the noise down, but you've woken the entire household. Come on. Let's make breakfast."

I was still in a complete daze when my mother said as she went out:

"What on earth have you got in your hair, it looks like a grain, and don't you go eating in your room, you've got crumbs in the corner of your mouth."

I ran my hand through my hair and looked: yes, it was a grain exactly like the ones we fed to the pigeons in St Mark's Square… had I really gone to Venice??? I licked the corner of my mouth to take off the crumbs my mother had mentioned, and I recognized the taste of the 'S' shaped biscuits.

I squeezed Elio in my arms and whispered in his ear:

"I'll never tell anyone our secret. Never. This trip has been brilliant, thank you for taking me, I'll keep our happy times in my heart for the rest of my life."

Before going down for breakfast with my family, I took out the box I kept under my bed and I put the grain of corn inside, next to the other souvenirs from my travels. Already in there was my key from Geneva, and a photo of Tess in her pretty hat in London.

How brilliant and interesting my life was! I ran out of my room shouting: "Yippee, I love life!" which made my brothers and sisters laugh. My father just looked at me, shaking his head. "Perhaps you should get more punishments, you seem full of beans this morning!"

Arthur
in Venice

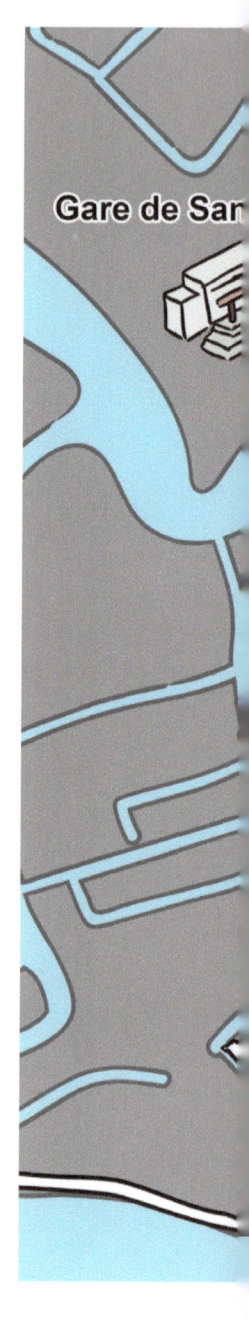

A Note about the Author

CAROLINE FERRERO MENUT
The ease with which children learn and their curiosity about everything around them has always fascinated me. As a mum and keen traveller, I was inspired to write these educational stories to encourage our children to discover new places with us, and it's exceeded all my expectations.

We have visited numerous villages, towns and countries, near or very far away, in the footsteps of imaginary characters invented for the occasion, with real enthusiasm, sense of fun and excitement.

A lawyer by profession, I'm familiar with writing as a means of expression, and in publishing this book, I wanted to share with other children the great pleasure of discovering new horizons and learning while having fun.

A note about the illustrator

NICOLE DEVALS

Nicole has loved drawing from as far back as she can remember. As a child, with her pencils and her keen powers of observation, she found she could express herself, find her place in the world and sketch, to the pleasure of everyone around her. Influenced by comic books, she quickly understood that the quality of a piece of work also comes from its images.

An outline of her life: in Lyon, Nicole went to Emile Cohl art school, which confirmed her decision to become an illustrator.

She carried on learning at a print shop as a graphic artist, a position she held for 12 years before launching herself out on her own. Affiliated to a publishing company, the print shop went on to see Nicole illustrate her first works.

Nowadays, she's using her skills as a graphic artist and illustrator on numerous projects. Her artistry finds expression as much in children's literature and learning support as in great international institutions.

Arthur's Travel Guides for Children

www.ingramcontent.com/pod-product-compliance
Lightning Source LLC
Chambersburg PA
CBHW061359090426

42743CB00002B/77